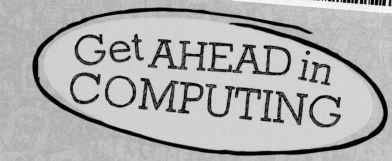

Get AHEAD in COMPUTING

Super SOCIAL MEDIA and Awesome ONLINE SAFETY

Clive Gifford

WAYLAND

First published in 2017 by Wayland
Copyright © Hodder and Stoughton, 2017

Wayland
Carmelite House
50 Victoria Embankment
London EC4Y 0DZ

Wayland Australia
Level 17/207 Kent Street
Sydney, NSW 2000

Produced for Wayland by
White-Thomson Publishing Ltd
www.wtpub.co.uk
01273 479982

Project Editor: Sonya Newland
Designer: Tim Mayer

A catalogue record for this title is available
from the British Library.

ISBN: 978 1 5263 0404 9

Printed in China

Wayland, part of Hachette Children's Group
and published by Hodder and Stoughton Limited

www.hachette.co.uk

All images courtesy of Shutterstock except:
iStock: p.20l (AnastasiaRasstrigina); Wikimedia: p.7t (LPS.1), p14 (secretlondon123)

Note to reader: Words highlighted in bold appear in the Glossary on page 30.

Contents

4   Keeping in Touch

6   Social Media History

8   Facebook

10   Instant Messaging and Microblogging

12   Sharing Snaps

14   Connecting to Social Media

16   How Information Spreads

18   The Business of Social Media

20   Signing Up and Starting Out

22   Keeping It Private

24   Smart, Safe Social Media

26   Social Media Issues

28   Cyberbullying

30   Glossary

31   Further Resources

32   Index

Keeping in Touch

Facebook, Snapchat, Twitter, Instagram … these and many other applications allow you to keep in touch with people, by sharing information such as photos or news using digital technology. These applications are known as social media and they've changed the way people work, live and communicate with others.

You can gain useful information and advice by asking questions and reading content provided by other members of a social media site.

You can share videos with ease on some social media sites.

Share and share alike

Traditional media, such as books and TV programmes, offer one-way information. They are created by a small number of people and then published or broadcast for more people to view. Social media is different because everyone can create and share content with each other. Content can be words, computer illustrations, photos and videos.

It's booming!

There are many reasons why social media has caught on. Most social media sites are free to use, and they make it quick and easy for people to stay connected with others. Keeping in touch with messages is often as simple as a few taps on a tablet, smartphone or other digital device.

Some social media apps allow you to alter pictures, using filters or special effects – such as turning a **selfie** into a dog! – before sharing them with others.

People post news about themselves and their families, as well as sharing national and local news stories over social media.

TRUE STORY

Tweets from the Top of the World. Adventurer Eric Larsen was the first person to tweet (send a message using Twitter) from the North Pole, in April 2010. Later that same year, he sent another tweet, this time from the top of Mount Everest, the highest mountain on Earth.

 ## Content kings and queens

Many types of social media help people produce content. This means that users do not need technical skills to create a personal page on a social media site or to share a photo to all their friends, for example.

You can comment on, like or sometimes even share someone else's content.

Social Media History

Social media is a common part of today's digital world, but it has a relatively short history. Although people were able to connect with one another using emails and messages in the 1980s, social media websites only blossomed in the 1990s and 2000s.

 ## Bulletin boards

The first elements of social media could be found on bulletin board systems (BBSs) in the late 1970s. These were mostly simple computer noticeboards to which users sent messages and files. They often did this by connecting their computer to a telephone line and making expensive long-distance calls.

 ## Online community

In 1995, GeoCities was launched. This offered people the chance to create their own simple homepage on the World Wide Web. All these homepages were stored on the GeoCities **server**. By the end of the 1990s, it was one of the most popular sites on the web.

Social media pioneers

In 1995, Classmates became one of the first social networks. It was used by school and college friends to keep in touch. SixDegrees.com followed in 1997, and was considered by many to be the first true social media site. At its peak it had 3.5 million users, but it closed in 2001. These sites were followed in the 2000s by Friends Reunited in the UK and Friendster, Myspace and others in the United States.

TRUE STORY

Short-Lived Social Site!
Wal-Mart launched The Hub as a social media site for teenagers in 2006. It lasted just 10 weeks before closing down!

LinkedIn

LinkedIn was designed to help professional people make connections rather than friends. The site allowed them to **upload** and share their CVs, find out about job opportunities and link with people in similar industries. By late 2016, when Microsoft bought LinkedIn for US$26.4 billion, it had more than 450 million members.

COMPUTER Hero!

Before modern social media, people often shared images and other file types by email. American programmer **Nathaniel Borenstein** created the code that allowed emails to carry these files, known as attachments. Before this, emails could only include a message in text. Borenstein's first two attachments were a photo and sound file of his barber-shop quartet singing!

How Much Time Do You Spend Online?

In 2016, the amount of time under-16s in the UK spent on the **Internet** overtook the time they spent watching television. Children in the UK now spend an average of three hours online per day according to the children's research agency Childwise.

Soaring social media

Social media really came into its own with the arrival of smartphones and tablets. These devices could link to the Internet without wires, which allowed people to post updates and share pictures and information while they were on the move. By the end of 2016, almost a third of the people on the planet used social media.

Facebook

The biggest and most popular social network of all, Facebook, began life in 2004 as thefacebook.com website at Harvard University. A student there, Mark Zuckerberg, created the website with some friends as a way for students to get in touch and learn more about each other.

Finding friends

Facebook allows users to search through its members for a person they know. If you send a 'friend request' and they accept, you are linked and can share information. What your friend writes appears in your news feed, and you can add your own comments to this activity. Your main workspace on Facebook is your Timeline, and you can post things on this using the 'What's on your mind?' box at the top of the page.

Facebook expands

By the end of 2005, Facebook was booming. It had spread to more than 2,000 colleges and over 25,000 high schools across the United States. Within three years, it boasted 100 million users. By late 2016, the company claimed an incredible 1.8 billion users. That's almost a quarter of the 7.4 billion people on the entire planet!

TRUE STORY

Separated at Birth! In 2013, two 25-year-old Facebook friends, Anaïs Bordier who lived in France and Samantha Futerman who lived in the United States, found out that they were twin sisters who had been born in South Korea but adopted by different families.

Like and more

Facebook's Like button allows users to agree with another user's post, or approve of an image or video that was shared, simply by clicking a button. Being able to Like other people's posts proved incredibly popular: in March 2013, an amazing 4.5 billion Likes were produced each day.

Facebook Live

In 2015, Facebook introduced a new feature. Facebook Live allowed users to stream video simply by tapping the Go Live button on their smartphone or tablet. Video taken by the device could be watched in real time by their friends on Facebook.

COMPUTER Hero!

Zuckerberg suffers from red-green colour blindness, which is why Facebook's colour scheme is blue.

Facebook creator **Mark Zuckerberg** was only 12 years old when he created his first social network, Zucknet, which connected members of his family. He continued **coding** as a teenager, creating Facemash — a site that allowed students to vote on which of them was most attractive. According to *Forbes* magazine, in 2016 Zuckerberg was worth a cool US$49.3 billion!

There are now six ways of reacting to Facebook content: Like, Love, Sad, Wow, Haha and Angry.

As of January 2017, the most Likes received by any one individual's personal page on Facebook was 118.6 million for Portuguese soccer star Cristiano Ronaldo.

Instant Messaging and Microblogging

Instant messaging (IM) and microblogging are forms of speedy social media, made up of brief messages. These allow information such as sports scores, news updates and meeting times and places to be passed on quickly.

Instant messaging

Instant messaging is a type of two-way chat using short text messages sent over the Internet or another computer network. The first worldwide messaging program, launched in 1996, was ICQ ('I Seek You'). Messaging programs are called clients, and Facebook Messenger, WhatsApp, Kik Messenger and Snapchat are among the best known.

Twitter

Launched in 2006, Twitter offers users the chance to make and share short messages called tweets. These contain up to 140 letters, numbers and symbols. They might seem similar to instant messages but tweets are public, last forever and can be searched for by anyone, not just members of Twitter.

Microblogging

Microblogging is a shorter version of a **blog**, in which people send short messages – usually just text or a link to a website. People use microblogs to share rapid updates on their day. Tumblr and Friendfeed are popular microblogging sites, but the most famous is Twitter.

Many celebrities use Twitter to create a more personal connection with their fans. The three most followed people on Twitter at the start of 2017 were all pop stars: Katy Perry, Justin Bieber and Taylor Swift.

Follower and following

If you 'follow' someone on Twitter, you receive all the tweets they post. The number of people you are following, as well as the number of followers you have yourself, are displayed at the top of your profile page. Most of this page is devoted to the feed where new, incoming tweets are displayed.

#HASHTAGS

A hashtag (#) is a tag used on Twitter and some other social media sites. It is used directly before a word or phrase in a tweet, and the words that follow are a sort of label attached to the tweet. For example, if you're tweeting about your new bike, you might include, #mountainbike or #age13birthday. Hashtags make it easier for users to find messages with a specific theme or content.

STRETCH YOURSELF

Tweet Without Joining Twitter!

Try to write clear, entertaining messages in no more than 140 characters to:

☞ tell people you have a new pet

☞ explain how you came top of the class in a test

☞ recommend that people read a particular book.

Think about how you can get your point across so that everyone can understand. Come up with one, two or three hashtag words to make each tweet easier to search for.

Sharing Snaps

Everyone likes to take photos of interesting things they see, their friends or even themselves (selfies). Many popular social media sites let you share your photos and, in some cases, your videos as well.

 ## Instagram

Instagram is a photo-sharing social media site used by more than 400 million people. It allows you to take photos that appear instantly on your profile, which can be shared with others. You can give your pictures different looks by selecting one of Instagram's photo filters.

Each person's profile lists the number of people following them on Instagram.

 ## Snapchat

Self-destructing photos are Snapchat's thing! People take a picture or very short video, then add a caption or maybe draw over the top of the image before sending it to another person. When opened, the recipient has 10 seconds to view the snap before it disappears. Snapchat has over 300 million users, who sent an average of 9,000 snaps every second in 2016!

 ## YouTube

The very first video shown on the world's most popular video-sharing site, YouTube, showed one of its three founders, Jawed Karim, visiting San Diego Zoo. Since its launch in 2005, YouTube has grown into an enormous collection of online videos, uploaded by the public.

Pinterest

An unusual image-sharing social media site, Pinterest lets people gather images from websites and pin them on their personal pinboard, which others can browse. Some people use Pinterest to organise pictures of a subject they're interested in, such as fashion or ancient Roman history. Other Pinterest users add images they have seen on other people's pinboards to their own, using the Re-pin feature.

COMPUTER Heroes!

Mike Krieger and **Kevin Systrom** founded Instagram in 2010, in California, USA. It was launched as a mobile-phone **app** later that year, and gained 100,000 users in its first week. In 2012, less than two years after its launch, Facebook bought Instagram for US$1 billion!

Flickr

Formed by Internet company Yahoo, Flickr allows users to share large numbers of photos, in galleries. It comes with a built-in app that lets people edit their photos, such as resizing them, making them brighter or darker, or adding special effects.

TRUE STORY

Top YouTuber! Internet celebrity PewDiePie (real name Felix Kjellberg) is the most followed person on YouTube. His channel of YouTube videos had 52 million subscribers at the start of 2017.

Connecting to Social Media

Social media works by letting people share their thoughts, news and digital files such as sound files or images. To do so, they must connect their device to a social media service.

Early connections

In the 1980s, computer users mostly shared files and messages by connecting their computer to a telephone line using a device called an acoustic coupler (below). Some of these operated at speeds thousands of times slower than today's Internet connections.

Getting online

Today, people usually connect with social media using the Internet or another computer network. An Internet connection may feature wires running from a home computer to a device called a router-modem. The modem part turns computer data into signals that can be sent down telephone lines. The router part creates a computer network, allowing different computers and devices in the home to link up.

Without wires

Many routers create a wireless area known as a **WiFi** zone or hotspot. This means that devices such as smartphones, tablets and some Smart TVs can connect to the Internet wirelessly. WiFi sends and receives radio signals to and from your digital devices.

Server farms

Social media companies sometimes use tens of thousands of servers to handle the huge amounts of information its members create. These servers are often grouped together in large centres known as server farms. Twitter has thousands of computers in a server farm in Atlanta that covers an area the size of 17 football fields.

TRUE STORY

Social Media in Space! Satellites whizzing through space in orbit around Earth can also link people to social media. In 2010, US astronaut T. J. Creamer sent the first live tweet from space. He wrote: 'Hello Twitterverse! We r now LIVE tweeting from the International Space Station.'

Go with the Flow

User
Someone sends a post to their social media account using their device. The device connects to the Internet wirelessly using a radio signal, and sends the message to the host.

Host
The social media site uses a series of powerful computers called servers. These act as the host, storing all the information, photos, videos and other files sent by its users. The host also sends information out from its servers to other social media users.

Receiver 1
Another social media user, connected to the Internet on their home computer, receives the message from the host.

Receiver 2
Using their smartphone, another person receives the poster's message and adds a comment. This is sent back to the host and then sent out to other social media users.

How Information Spreads

When you join social media, you make connections with others. These people are often referred to as 'friends', even if they are not friends in the traditional sense. You may not know them in real life!

 Going viral

If you post a message to all your friends, some of them may share it with their friends – not all of whom will be on your friends list. Those friends of friends may then share it with their own connections, and so on. In this way, messages and information travel through social networks widely and rapidly. A post that becomes really well known and popular in a short space of time is said to have 'gone viral'.

Linking social media

Many people link their different social media accounts. This means that what they post on Instagram, for example, can be seen on other sites such as Flickr or Facebook. Accounts with the same email address can be linked so that posting an update on one will automatically post it on the others.

If each of those 100 people share the post with their list of 40 friends, it would then be seen by 4,000 more people!

Five of Jenny's friends, all of whom have 20 friends on their list, comment on Jenny's post. The post and comments are now seen by 100 more people.

Jenny enjoys an ice cream and posts to all her 20 friends on social media to let them know.

Now trending...

Popular posts or links that gather a lot of views, shares, retweets or reposts are often gathered together in a **trending** panel on social media sites. This allows users not only to see what their own friends have posted, but also what's hot right now.

TRUE STORY

Animal-lovers. Animal photos, videos and stories are popular subjects on social media. An image of a baby panda in China sneezing loudly and startling its mother went viral. By the start of 2017, it had been viewed on YouTube over 221 million times!

STRETCH YOURSELF

On the Level
Pick a famous person in history. Imagine what sort of posts, photos and comments they would have made if today's social media had been around at the time. Try to think of how the different social media might be used to communicate different things. For example:

☞ Design a simple Facebook profile of a famous figure from history.

☞ Write some tweets from that person and their friends or enemies.

☞ Draw several photographs they might have sent to social media if smartphones had been around.

Will.i.am Shakespeare

The Business of Social Media

AMAZING ONLINE DISCOUNTS!

CYBER MONDAY

Nearly all social media is free, but it can cost media companies a lot of money to build and maintain their sites. So how do they cover these costs?

 Advertisers and advertising

The main way that social media companies make money is by charging other companies to advertise on their pages. Advertising is big business in the digital world: more than a third of all advertising spending in the United States in 2016 was on the Internet. In the same year, Instagram was paid over US$2 billion by advertisers.

TYPES OF ONLINE ADVERTISING

➪ Display adverts often appear at the top of a screen or in a bar running down the side of a page. Social media companies may charge advertisers by how many of their members click on these adverts, which take them to the advertiser's website.

➪ Some stories or posts that are sponsored by companies are placed on social media.

➪ Apps are designed containing lots of advertising. These are sometimes called **app-verts**.

➪ Some celebrities or experts are paid to advertise and promote a product or service on their own social media pages.

Selling your habits

Social media companies, such as Twitter and Facebook, also make money by selling the data (information) that they collect about their users. This is known as 'data licensing'. These companies know your age, location and some of your interests. They may also know which celebrities, bands or sports teams you follow. This information is important to advertisers, who use it to target their products.

Not quite free

Joining a social media site may be free, but users sometimes have to pay for certain features or additional benefits. This is called **freemium**. Flickr, for example, offers users a certain amount of space to upload and share their photos. To get unlimited space, users have to pay for the 'premium' service.

STRETCH YOURSELF

Play Admongo
Learn more about advertising, both online and all around you, by playing the Admongo platform game by the Federal Trade Commission (FTC). Just type the address below into your web **browser**.

☞ https://game.admongo.gov/

As you avoid the minions and collect the adverts, you will discover more about how advertising works.

TRUE STORY

Money-spinners! Facebook makes some of its money from the games hosted on its site. A lot of people play these games. The top 10 games on Facebook in October 2016 — including 8 Ball Pool, Pet Rescue Saga and Clash of Clans — were played by 340 million people during that month.

Signing Up and Starting Out

Social media sites all work in different ways and have their own rules. Most insist that you become a member before you can use their services. This means giving details about yourself, so always ask an adult before you sign up to anything!

 ## Profile page

Most social media sites expect you to complete a profile page with basic information about yourself. Be careful what you say here. Mention some of your likes and interests in general, and the region you're from, in order to connect with like-minded people, but don't give specifics such as your address.

Age limit

Many social media sites, including Facebook, Instagram, Pinterest, Tumblr, Reddit and Snapchat, set a minimum age of 13 for people to become members. On other sites, including WhatsApp, the minimum age is 16. These limits are there to protect children, because some users may try to share information that is not suitable for younger people.

Some people include a personal photo on their profile page, but others prefer to use a cartoon or made-up image to represent themselves instead. This is called an **avatar**.

COMPUTER Hero!

Californian kid **Zach Marks** was twice removed from Facebook after he set up accounts before he was 13. Instead of sulking, Zach decided to create his own social network for kids, with his father's help. Grom Social was launched in 2012 and allows children (who have to sign up with a parent) to chat, share videos, play games against one another and get help with their homework. By 2016, the site had over 3.5 million members.

 Social media for tweens

Today, there are plenty of fun, safe social media sites for kids. Kidzworld is one of the most popular. Members can swap TV and movie reviews, send messages in chat rooms and play online arcade games against each other. Other sites, such as Kuddle, allow children to share photos in a safe way or, like PlayKids Talk, offer instant messaging.

 **STRETCH YOURSELF**

Design Your Own Social Network
Grab some paper, pens and even friends to help you design your own social network. Think about these questions:

☞ What would you call it?

☞ What features would it offer members?

☞ How would you make it easy for members to create and share content?

☞ How would it be different from existing social media?

☞ How would you make it safe and suitable for young people to use?

Keeping It Private

You may have to give your details to a social media company to join, but that doesn't mean you have to tell everyone on the site everything about you!

What is personal data?

Personal data is anything about you – from your address and age to the school you go to, the names of your brothers and sisters, what your parents do for a living and where they work. You should not share this information on social media sites.

Home alone

Your personal details may not seem important, but they can be misused by others. For example, many burglaries occur after someone posts on social media that they are going away, revealing that their home will be empty. Smartphones and many tablets can pinpoint your position on the planet using GPS or other satellite navigation systems. If you leave this option on and it appears in your status updates, everyone knows when you're not at home!

Password power

Your password to a social media site is your first line of defence when it comes to privacy. It's something you probably rarely think about – until you forget it! If someone has your password and other details, they may be able to log in to your account and pretend to be you on a social network.

Privacy settings

If a social media site has no privacy settings, then people you don't know may be able to see all your content. Within many social media sites there are settings that allow you to decide how much or how little you share with the outside world. For example, Facebook has a range of privacy settings for photos and messages. You can choose from:

- Public: anyone can see this material including people not on Facebook.
- Friends: only your Facebook friends can view.
- Custom: you can pick and choose precisely which people get to view your content.
- Only Me: for your eyes only.

STRONG AND WEAK PASSWORDS

Passwords are categorised by strength. A weak password is one that other people could work out quite easily. It might be a simple sequence of letters or numbers such as 1234567 or WXYZ, or it might be your name or the year you were born. Follow these tips to keep your data safe:

 Mix numbers and upper- and lower-case letters to create a strong password.

 Use a different password for your email and each social media site you use.

 Never tell other members of a social media site your password.

STRETCH YOURSELF

Create a Password
Try to come up with a bulletproof password – one that even your best friend won't be able to work out. If you struggle, try using an online password generator such as https://identitysafe.norton.com/password-generator/. Type in the number of characters you want your new password to contain, and whether it should include numbers and punctuation symbols. The site will create a password for you in a flash!

Smart, Social Safe Media

Going on the Internet to connect with friends and share content can be great fun … especially if you remember to be smart and thoughtful.

 Be a social media star

Here are five top tips to succeed on social media.

1. Have patience. Building a network of friends online can take time. Don't worry if someone you know won't link with you. It's probably not personal – they may simply prefer to have a small number of connections, or they may use social media only occasionally.

2. Stay positive. Even if you don't agree with someone else's opinion or interests, don't be rude or make fun of them. Studies show that people who are friendly and positive often gain more followers and friends online.

3. Be interesting. Don't just post what you had for lunch – unless it was really unusual or you have eaten somewhere strange! If something funny happens at school or at the weekend, take your time to write it up in an amusing way. However, do not give the real names or any personal details about the other people involved.

4. Be helpful. If you're asked questions on social media, answer them politely and quickly (as long as they're not asking for personal data). If you see someone is struggling with something you can help with, do so. The chances are you'll need help with something before long.

5. Stay active. Post and update regularly, as this is more likely to attract friends or followers. But don't bombard people or become obsessed with going online every day. Staying active also means getting outside and away from social media!

24

Comment class

Acting in a polite, friendly way on social media will gain you respect and avoid problems. Here are some do's and don'ts:

- **Do** consider how what you say might affect others. Do people really want or need to know what you're about to share?
- **Don't** type things or share images that other people might find offensive.
- **Do** ask permission before posting or sharing pictures or details of someone.

- **Don't** get upset or angry and post something you may regret later. If you feel yourself turning red, take a break from your computer, smartphone or tablet and go and do something else that you enjoy.

TRUE STORY

There For All to See. A 2016 survey in the United States showed that 60 per cent of employers now look back over a person's social media content when they apply for a job. The applicant's **digital footprint** sometimes influences whether they get the job or not. A large number of colleges also review students' social media use.

Digital footprint

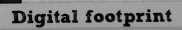

Remember – every time you go on social media, visit websites or send chat-room messages, you are increasing your digital footprint. This is all the evidence of your time online, and includes every word, photo and video you've uploaded. All this material continues to exist and may be accessed by others far into the future.

Social Media Issues

Social media is wildly popular, but this popularity has attracted some people intent on causing upset and harm. These people often target children and teenagers.

 ## Not who they are

Many people like social media because they can hide behind their username and avatar – they can pretend to be someone else. This is often harmless fun, but sometimes it is more sinister. Occasionally, adults pretend to be children to lure their online 'friends' to meet them. Always remember that someone might not be who they say they are.

 ## Trolls

Trolls are people who deliberately upset or disrupt others online by saying nasty things or perhaps giving advice that backfires. Trolls also try to provoke arguments. If you are trolled, don't respond to it, but do let a parent or teacher know.

 ## Griefers

Griefers are similar to trolls, but they operate in online games. They try to spoil another gamer's enjoyment. They might do this by stopping them playing, or by sabotaging their chances of doing well in the game.

Many griefers have damaged or destroyed other players' buildings in Minecraft, purely to cause upset.

NEVER agree to meet someone you only know on social media and not in real life without a parent present.

Unfriending and blocking

If someone keeps bothering you, by trolling you or sending content that you don't want, you do not have to leave your favourite social media site or create a new account. Some social media sites allow you to remove the link between you and the other person.

On Facebook, you can unfriend someone so that they are no longer part of your network. You can also block them. This stops you both from seeing each other's comments. It means the other person cannot add you as a friend or invite you to events. If you later sort out your issues, you can unblock them.

Feeling uncomfortable

If you receive something that upsets you or makes you feel uncomfortable, such as violent videos, sexual images or disturbing stories and messages, stop looking or reading. Leave your computer or device and talk to a parent, a teacher or another adult you trust.

Collecting Evidence

One of the most important things you can do if you are trolled, or sent rude or inappropriate messages or images, is to collect and store all the material as evidence. If you don't have a printer, you can take a **screenshot**:

Apple iPhone and iPad: Press and hold the Sleep/Wake button on the top or side, then press and release the Home button. The screenshot will appear in the Camera Roll of the Photos app.

Android: Many Android phones and tablets allow you to take a screenshot by pressing the Power button and either the Volume Down or the Home button at the same time.

Windows 8 and 10: Pressing both the Windows and Print Screen keys at the same time will capture the entire screen.

Windows 7: Use the Snipping tool found in All Programs when you press Windows' Start button (usually found in the bottom left corner of the screen). This will call up a rectangle that can be enlarged to full screen by dragging on the corner with the mouse.

Cyber-bullying

Cyberbullying is the use of technology to harass, threaten or embarrass another person, usually a child or teenager. The cyberbully may repeatedly use text messages, instant messaging, emails and social media.

What is cyberbullying?

According to a 2015 survey, almost one in six of all American schoolchildren reported they were victims of cyberbullying. What sorts of things happened to them?

- The bully constantly sent rude or disturbing messages or images.

- The bully wrote things about the victim that were untrue and shared them with other people on social media.

- The bully posted online lots of rude or embarrassing jokes or pictures about the victim.

- The bully shared with everyone personal information or secrets they had been told by the victim in the past.

- The bully threatened the victim, saying that they were going to confront or hurt them.

Tackling cyberbullies

There are a number of things you can do to combat cyberbullying:

- Don't blame yourself. It is the cyber-bully who has a problem – not you.

- Tell an adult you trust, such as a parent, teacher or carer.

- Don't reply to the bully or try to retaliate by sending similar messages and posts about them. This will only make things worse and may lead to you becoming a cyberbully as well.

- Keep all the bullying posts, messages and images. Store all the evidence of bullying by saving, printing or making screenshots (see page 27) of all the bully's messages and posts.

- Block the bully from any social media accounts you use (see page 27).

The accidental cyberbully

You may become part of a cyberbullying problem without realising it. Liking or sharing messages or images that could be hurtful or embarrassing can make someone feel that they are alone and being ganged up against. Always ask yourself how you would feel if it happened to you. If you think you may have upset someone in this way, apologise to them. You'll both feel better!

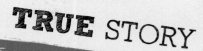

TRUE STORY

Paying the Price.

Cyberbullying is a crime in many countries. In 2009, 18-year-old Keeley Houghton was sent to prison for three months for bullying another teenage girl on Facebook. This was one of the first prison sentences handed out to a cyberbully in the UK.

STRETCH YOURSELF

Get to Grips with Cyberbullying

Visit the Digizen website by typing the address below into your web browser.

☞ http://www.digizen.org/resources/digizen-game.aspx

There, you can take on a character, and role-play an entire day at school to see how cyberbullying can occur and the sorts of choices people make to ignore or tackle it.

Glossary

apps Software programs downloaded and run on a smartphone or tablet.

app-verts Adverts designed to be placed in apps and computer games.

avatar An image used to represent a person online (often not an actual photo of them).

blog Short for web log – a list of diary or journal entries posted on a webpage for others to read.

browser A type of program used to view websites on the World Wide Web.

coding Writing the lines of code in a program that make a computer or other device work.

cyberbullying The use of digital technology, such as text messages, social media and instant messaging, to harass, threaten or bully someone.

digital footprint All the traces of your time online on social media and computer networks, including posts, photos and messages.

freemium A pricing technique by companies, where the user gets the basic version of a site or application free of charge, but must pay for additional features.

griefer Someone who deliberately tries to spoil an online game for other users.

Instant messaging (IM) A type of direct communication using text between two or more people.

Internet A network that connects millions of computers all over the world.

screenshot A picture of the screen on a computer or digital device.

selfie A photograph that you take of yourself using your mobile phone.

server A computer system in a network that sends information to a number of computers on the network.

trending A topic, such as a news story or funny image, that is one of the most talked about on a social media network at the time.

troll Someone who deliberately sends upsetting or annoying messages on social media to disrupt a group or start arguments.

upload To send a computer file from one computer to another or, if connected to a network, sending the file to the network for others to view, use and share.

WiFi Wireless local area network technology that allows people to connect computers and other digital devices to one another and to the Internet.

Further Resources

Books

The Quick Expert's Guide To Safe Social Networking by Anita Naik (Wayland, 2015)

Texts, Tweets, Trolls and Teens: A Survival Guide for Social Networking by Anita Naik (Wayland, 2014)

Bullies, Cyberbullies and Frenemies by Michele Elliott (Wayland, 2013)

Social Networking: Big Business on Your Computer by Nick Hunter (Franklin Watts, 2015)

Websites

https://www.thinkuknow.co.uk/
A great site for tips and knowledge on staying safe online and when using social networks, brought to you by the National Crime Agency.

http://www.pepperitmarketing.com/facebook/evolution-social-media
Watch this interesting 90-second video on the history of social media, from CNBC.

http://computer.howstuffworks.com/internet/social-networking/networks/facebook.htm
Lots of information from How Stuff Works on how Facebook operates.

http://www.bbc.co.uk/cbbc/curations/stay-safe
Great advice and videos on how to stay safe online, including when using social media.

Index

a
acoustic coupler 14
advertising 18, 19
age restrictions 20, 21
animals 17
app 13, 27
app-verts 18
attachments 7
avatar 20, 26

b
Bieber, Justin 10
blocking 27
blog 10
Bordier, Anaïs 8
Borenstein, Nathaniel 7
bulletin board 6

c
celebrities 10, 18, 19
chat room 21, 25
children 7, 20, 21, 26
Clash of Clans 19
Classmates 6
code 7
coding 9
companies 18, 19
computer 6, 10, 14, 15, 25, 27
content 4, 5, 23, 24, 27
Creamer, T. J. 15
cyberbullying 28–29

d
data licensing 19
digital footprint 25
Digizen 29

e
8 Ball Pool 19
email 6, 7, 23, 28
Everest, Mount 5

f
Facebook 4, 8–9, 13, 16, 17, 19, 20,
   21, 23, 27, 29
Facebook Live 9
Facebook Messenger 10
Facemash 9
filters 5, 12
Flickr 13, 16, 19
followers 11, 13, 24
freemium 19
Friendfeed 10
friends 16, 23, 24, 26, 27
Friends Reunited 6
Friendster 6
Futerman, Samantha 8

g
games 19, 21, 26
GeoCities 6
GPS 22
griefers 26
Grom Social 21

h
Harvard University 8
hashtag 11
homepage 6
host 15
Houghton, Keeley 29
Hub, The 6

i
ICQ 10
Instagram 4, 12, 13, 16, 18, 20
instant messaging (IM) 10, 21, 28
Internet 7, 10, 13, 14, 15, 18, 24

k
Karim, Jawed 12
Kik Messenger 10
Krieger, Mike 13
Kuddle 21

l
Larsen, Eric 5
Liking 9, 29
LinkedIn 7
links 7, 10, 14, 15, 16, 17, 24, 27

m
Marks, Zach 21
microblogging 10
Microsoft 7
modem 14
Myspace 6

n
news 4, 5, 10, 14
news feed 8
North Pole 5

p
password 22, 23
Perry, Katy 10
personal data 22, 24
personal page 5, 9
Pet Rescue Saga 19
PewDiePie 13
photos 4, 5, 7, 12–13, 15, 17, 19, 20,
   21, 23, 25
Pinterest 13, 20
PlayKids Talk 21
posts 7, 9, 15, 16, 17, 18, 22, 24, 25,
   28
privacy 22–23
profile 11, 12, 17, 20

r
radio signal 14, 15
Reddit 20
Ronaldo, Cristiano 9
router 14
rules 20

s
satellites 15, 22
screenshot 27, 28
selfie 5, 12
server 6, 15
SixDegrees.com 6
Smart TV 14
smartphone 4, 7, 9, 14, 15, 17, 22, 25
Snapchat 4, 10, 12, 20
sound file 7, 14
Swift, Taylor 10
Systrom, Kevin 13

t
tablet 4, 7, 9, 14, 22, 25, 27
teenagers 6, 9, 26, 28
telephone line 14
traditional media 4
trending 17
trolls 26, 27
Tumblr 10, 20
Twitter 4, 5, 10, 11, 15, 19

u
unfriending 27
username 26

v
videos 4, 9, 15, 21, 25

w
Wal-Mart 6
WhatsApp 10, 20
WiFi 14
World Wide Web 6

y
Yahoo 13
YouTube 12, 13, 17

z
Zuckerberg, Mark 8, 9
Zucknet 9

TITLES IN THE SERIES

 COMPUTING and CODING in the Real World — Clive Gifford

Computing All Around Us
Input and Output
All About Algorithms
Real-World Algorithms
Sensors
Coding Decisions
In Control
Barcodes and Stock Control
Where Am I?
Money Matters
Working with Robots
3D Printing
The Internet of Things

 GREAT Games — Clive Gifford

Fun on the Screen
Early Computer Games
Types of Games
Storyboards
Game Assets
Game Characters
The Game World
Game Rules and Features
Coding Games
Decision Time!
Controlling Games
Keeping Score
Testing and Launching

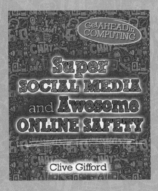 Super SOCIAL MEDIA and Awesome ONLINE SAFETY — Clive Gifford

Keeping in Touch
Social Media History
Facebook
Instant Messaging and
  Microblogging
Sharing Snaps
Connecting to Social Media
How Information Spreads
The Business of Social Media
Signing Up and Starting Out
Keeping It Private
Smart, Safe Social Media
Social Media Issues
Cyberbullying

 WEBPAGE Design — Clive Gifford

Welcome to the World Wide Web
How the Web Works
The Web Designer's Toolkit
A Selection of Sites
Welcome to HTML
Creating a Page
Adding Images
Jumping Around
Site, Right!
Doing It in Style
Content Management Systems
Design Over time
Added Features

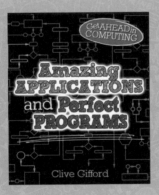 Amazing APPLICATIONS and Perfect PROGRAMS — Clive Gifford

Program Explosion
Operating Systems
Popular Operating Systems
Interface to Face
Data and Circuits
Files in Style
Getting Organised
It's the Business
Text Success
Words and Picture
Sounds and Music
Games, Games, Games
App Attack!

 Awesome ALGORITHMS and Creative CODING — Clive Gifford

Coding your World
Algorithms in Action
Ones and Zeros
Mind your Language
Languages for Learning
Scratch!
Accurate Algorithms
Get in Step
Decisions, Decisions
Go with the Flow
Going Loopy
A Bug's Life
Coding Careers

 The Science of COMPUTERS — Clive Gifford

A World of Computers
The Incredible
  Shrinking Computer
Here's the Hardware
Let's Look Inside
Data and Circuits
Memory Matters
Imput Devices
More Input Devices
Sounds Amazing
Picture Perfect
Computer Gaming
Mega and Mini Machines

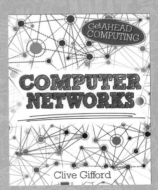 COMPUTER NETWORKS — Clive Gifford

Networks All Around Us
Let's Connect
The Internet
World Wide Web
Web Wonders
A World of Websites
Search Engines
Search and Filter
You've Got Mail
Social Networks
Danger Danger!
Keep It To Yourself